Backyard Insects

by Millicent E. Selsam
and Ronald Goor

A CITATION PRESS BOOK
published by Scholastic, Inc.

SCHOLASTIC INC.
New York Toronto London Auckland Sydney

Additional Photos

Page 15 (bottom), 31 – Bruce Coleman; Page 24 – Dr. Lincoln P. Brower

ISBN 0-590-42256-1

Text copyright © 1981 by Millicent E. Selsam. Photographs copyright © 1981 by Ronald Goor. All rights reserved. Published by Scholastic Inc.

21 20 19 18 17 16 15 14   6 7 8 9/9 0/0

Printed in the U.S.A.

For Margaret Amanda Selsam

Millicent E. Selsam

For Alex, Danny, and Nancy

Ron Goor

4

Did you know that there may be more than
a thousand different kinds of insects
in your own backyard?
They live in the grass, on bushes and trees,
under rocks, and in the soil.

Hungry birds, frogs, lizards, and spiders
are always searching for these insects to eat.
But insects can escape from them
in surprising ways.

Hidden Insects

Can you find the three moths in these pictures?
Can a hungry bird find them easily?

One looks like bark.

One looks like part of a branch.

One looks like the forest floor it is resting on.

Look for twigs with legs and you will find
the walking sticks in these pictures.
One is green and matches the green twigs.

The other is brown and matches the brown twigs
of the tree it feeds on.

Is it a young leaf? Suddenly it moves.
Now you know it is really an insect.
It is called a planthopper.
If you get too close, it will jump
to the opposite side of the stem.
The veins on its wings are just like
the veins of a young leaf.

This insect sings all night.
During the day, it sits quietly.
It looks like a leaf too.
It is a katydid.
Can you find it?

You really have to look three or four times
to find the stinkbug resting on this bark.
It is very hard to find.
It also gives off a bad odor
that helps keep enemies away.

Some caterpillars are hard to find too.

Find the one that looks like the rolled edge of a leaf.

Find the one that looks like a spike of grass.

Find the caterpillar that looks like the leaves of a plant.

Find the one that looks like a twig.

Find the one that looks like the flowers
it is resting on.

15

This bagworm caterpillar carries its bag around
the way a snail carries its shell. The bag is made of twigs
and pieces of leaves held together by silk.

Look at the top of this photo. See how
the caterpillar comes part way out of the bag
to munch on green leaves.

After feeding all summer,

it attaches the bag to a twig.

There it changes into an adult moth.

A frothy bunch of bubbles is fastened
to a tender plant stem.

An insect is hidden inside.

It sucks plant juices hour after hour

and gives off the soapy liquid that covers it.

It is called a froghopper.

When insects are hidden

or look like the place where they live,

they are protected from their enemies.

This kind of protection is called natural camouflage (kam-a-flaj).

Insects with "Warning" Colors

Not all insects are hard to find.
Many of them have very bright colors.
Their enemies can easily see them,
but they do not go after them.
The bright bands of black and yellow
on bees and wasps are "warning" colors
that give the message "I sting."

Toads try to catch honeybees.
But after they get stung a few times,
they leave them alone
even though they are very hungry.

bee

wasp

Brightly colored ladybird beetles give the message
"I taste bad," and are not eaten by many birds.

The monarch butterfly has orange and black colors.

The colors "warn" that this butterfly is bitter and poisonous.

If a bird swallows a monarch butterfly,

it gets sick and throws up.

After that, it does not try to eat monarch butterflies.

The monarch butterfly gets its poison
from a plant called milkweed.
It feeds on this plant when it is a caterpillar.
The caterpillar shows "warning" colors too,
and is also poisonous.

milkweed beetle

Many other insects with "warning" colors live
on plants in the milkweed family.

Look at the bright colors of the milkweed beetle,
the milkweed bug,
and the caterpillar of the harlequin moth.

Birds leave these poisonous insects alone
once they have tried them.

Milkweed bug

harlequin moth

Copycat Insects

Look at the two butterflies in the pictures.
One is a monarch butterfly.
The other is a viceroy butterfly that looks almost exactly like it.
There is a small difference — a dark line across
the viceroy's hind wings.
Can you find it?

The caterpillars of the viceroys do not feed on milkweed,
so they do not have any milkweed poison in them.
But birds leave viceroys alone because they are "copies"
or "mimics" of the monarchs.

monarch butterfly

viceroy butterfly

Here are three insects that mimic the colors of wasps.
One is a fly.

One is a beetle.

One is a moth.

All are harmless.

But their enemies avoid these wasp colors.

Scary Insects

Some insects flash bright spots of color
that look like eyes.

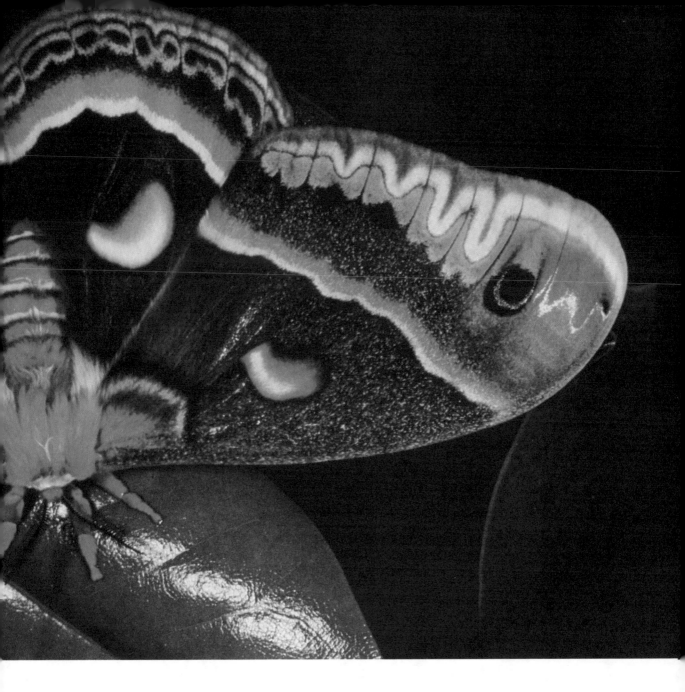

The cecropia silkworm moth spreads its wings.
Suddenly it becomes a giant face with big "eyes."

Even caterpillars flash "eyes."
This caterpillar of the swallowtail butterfly
can suddenly show an enormous pair of false eyes.
The false eyes are just spots of color on the caterpillar's skin.
But these spots frighten away many birds, because
a bird's own enemies — owls, cats, and hawks —
have such eyes.

A swallowtail's real eyes are tiny.
They are on the sides of the head
in front of the false eyes.

Birds may stay away from this click beetle too,
because the patches of color on its back
look like big eyes.

The click beetle has still another way of protecting itself from enemies.

When it is touched, it gives a loud click.

Then it tucks up its legs and drops to the ground.

It usually lands on its back.

It lies still for a few minutes.

Then, suddenly, click! — it snaps into the air and lands on its feet.

It may get away before the bird picks it up.

Imagine coming face to face with this monster
while climbing your favorite hickory tree.
It is called the hickory horned devil.
It can get to be seven inches long.
It can get to be as fat as a big cigar.
It also has eight long, black-tipped, orange horns.
When attacked, this caterpillar whips its horns
from side to side.
Most birds leave and look for another insect meal.

Insects with Two Heads?

Will this grey hairstreak butterfly fly away
to the left or to the right?
Where is its head?
When attacked, the butterfly darts off.
Often it leaves its enemy with a piece of wing
instead of its head.

Insects have so many ways to escape,
you might wonder — are they ever found and eaten?
They are.
But the ones that are hidden
        or have "warning" colors
        or look like bad-tasting insects
        or scare off their enemies
are the ones who live the longest.
They lay the most eggs that grow up
into insects like themselves.
These insects *survive* better than the ones
that do not have such protection.

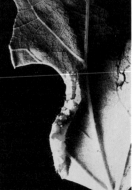